Making the Impossible Possible

MAKING THE IMPOSSIBLE POSSIBLE

❖ ❖ ❖ ❖ ❖

*The Six Historic Campaigns That
Laid the Foundation for Kosen-rufu*

❖ ❖ ❖ ❖ ❖

SELECTIONS FROM THE WRITINGS OF

DAISAKU IKEDA

World Tribune
Press

Published by World Tribune Press
A division of the SGI-USA
606 Wilshire Blvd.
Santa Monica, CA 90401

Cover and interior design by Gopa & Ted2, Inc.

26 25 24 23 22   1 2 3 4 5

ISBN: 978-1-944604-55-4

Library of Congress Control Number: 2021952057

Contents

◆ ◆ ◆ ◆ ◆ ◆

Editor's Note   vii

Prologue: Making My Mentor's Vow My Own   1

An Ode to My Mentor, Josei Toda   5

Kamata Campaign: February 1952   9

Bunkyo Chapter Campaign: April 1953   25

Sapporo Summer Campaign: August 1955   37

Kansai Campaign: January to May 1956   49

Yamaguchi Campaign:
October/November 1956 and January 1957   65

Arakawa Campaign: August 1957   83

Editor's Note

❖ ❖ ❖ ❖ ❖ ❖

In 1951, today's multimillion-member worldwide Buddhist association the Soka Gakkai was a tiny group of just some three thousand people trying to make their way in postwar Japan.

On May 3 that year, Josei Toda became the organization's second president and, determined to eliminate misery in Japan and the world, declared that he would realize a membership of 750,000 households before he died.

Making the Impossible Possible chronicles six trailblazing campaigns that Mr. Toda's young disciple Daisaku Ikeda led to make that goal a reality in less than seven years. By doing so, he opened the way for all members to deepen their conviction in faith, develop a sense of real joy and happiness, and trigger a new wave of expansion.

To this day, these pioneering campaigns continue to inspire Soka Gakkai members all around the world, providing invaluable guidance and memorable lessons. Most importantly, these stories lead us to believe that, like Shin'ichi Yamamoto (Mr. Ikeda's character in *The New Human Revolution*), if we keep our mentor in our hearts, no target is too high and no goal impossible to achieve.

This book draws mainly from *The New Human Revolution* and includes passages from other writings of Mr. Ikeda. World Tribune Press editors express our appreciation to the editors of Eternal Ganges Press in India for conceiving of and researching this valuable reference.

We've updated *The New Human Revolution* text to match the

most recent translations and printings of these volumes that were updated between 2019–21.

The citations most commonly used in this book have been abbreviated as follows:

- LSOC, page number(s) refers to *The Lotus Sutra and Its Opening and Closing Sutras,* translated by Burton Watson (Soka Gakkai: Tokyo, 2009).

- NHR, volume number, page number(s) refers to *The New Human Revolution,* updated editions from 2019–21.

- OTT, page number(s) refers to *The Record of the Orally Transmitted Teachings,* translated by Burton Watson (Tokyo: Soka Gakkai, 2004).

- WND, page number(s) refers to *The Writings of Nichiren Daishonin,* vol. 1 (WND-1) (Soka Gakkai: Tokyo, 1999) and vol. 2 (WND-2) (Soka Gakkai: Tokyo, 2006).

JAPAN

SAPPORO
ATSUTA
OTARU
HOKKAIDO
YUBARI

ICHINOSEKI
SADO
ISLAND
HONSHU
NIIGATA
SENDAI

KARUIZAWA
TOCHIGI

YAMAGUCHI
HIROSHIMA
OSAKA
MOUNT FUJI ▲
TOKYO
ARAKAWA
BUNKYO
KAMATA

SAKAI
AWA
IZU PENINSULA
SHIKOKU
SHIMODA

YAME

NAGASAKI
KANSAI

KYUSHU

WHERE THE CAMPAIGNS WERE FOUGHT

Map not to scale

Prologue:
Making My Mentor's Vow My Own

—————————— ♦ ♦ ♦ ♦ ♦ ♦ —— ——————————

At his inauguration as second president of the Soka Gakkai, which then had only around three thousand members, Josei Toda boldly vowed to realize a membership of 750,000 households. This towering goal was achieved in just six and a half years, thanks to the tireless efforts of the young Daisaku Ikeda, who made his mentor's heart his own and strove with unwavering determination to realize his mentor's vision.

AT HIS INAUGURATION as second Soka Gakkai president, Mr. Toda declared: "I will through my own efforts reach the membership goal of 750,000 households. Should I fail to do so, don't hold a funeral for me."

The majority of his disciples at that time, however, dismissed this important declaration—giving voice to the great vow he would devote his life to—as little more than a fantasy. The Soka Gakkai's newspaper, the *Seikyo Shimbun*, didn't even report his statement. Arrogant leaders, thinking that they knew better than their mentor, prevented its publication, not wishing to have an unachievable goal set down in print for posterity.

When Mr. Toda became president in May 1951, the monthly propagation goal of even the top chapters was a mere fifty households. But I realized that the path of a disciple is to make the vision of one's mentor a reality, no matter how challenging it might be. As Mr. Toda's disciple, his vow became my vow, and achieving it became my personal mission.

But propagation efforts throughout the organization failed to advance. In fact, in their hearts, everyone had given up. The veteran leaders did nothing but lament and moan about the thick wall that loomed before them and blocked the way to growth. I, however, saw it as a time ripe for action, and I leaped onto the main battlefield of kosen-rufu as the chapter advisor of Tokyo's Kamata Chapter.

This happened in the cold month of February 1952, the month of Mr. Toda's fifty-second birthday. I proclaimed Mr. Toda's message far and wide. I urged the members to follow the path of mentor and disciple. This is because when we align our hearts with the spirit of our mentor for kosen-rufu, the wisdom and courage innate to the Bodhisattvas of the Earth well forth within us.

Seeking to respond to Mr. Toda, the members joined me with renewed determination and set to work courageously. Our efforts brought us joy, hope, adventure, and energy. Everyone eagerly took part. And in one dramatic sweep, Kamata achieved the previously unheard-of goal of 201 new households in a single month. We realized that if we tried, we could succeed. A decisive breakthrough toward realizing Mr. Toda's membership goal of 750,000 households had been made. Kamata had triumphed! Great progress toward victory in my hometown of Tokyo had begun.

The Lotus Sutra teaches that the Buddha has the powers to "understand the way, open up the way, and preach the way" (see LSOC, 135). We who uphold the Mystic Law can also give expression to these powers.

As Mr. Toda's direct disciple, I visited areas throughout Tokyo and Japan, including Joto (eastern Tokyo), Bunkyo, Sapporo, Osaka, Kansai, Yamaguchi, Chugoku, Arakawa, and Katsushika. Everywhere I went, I opened a bright new path for kosen-rufu and unfailingly raised a victory banner of mentor and disciple. Each day saw incredibly difficult challenges. Nothing was ever easy. It was a struggle to achieve the seemingly impossible, to realize a feat that would astonish everyone.

What was the main cause for my success in that struggle? In short, it was that my heart was always one with my mentor. I reported on everything to Mr. Toda and received his guidance. I cannot count the times that I got off the train at Meguro, the station nearest to where he lived, and dashed to his home to report to him on the latest developments.

I also constantly asked myself, what would Mr. Toda do, what would he say if he saw me now? Was I behaving in a way that I could be proud of if he were watching? As I exerted myself wholeheartedly, I would picture in my mind Mr. Toda sometimes nodding in smiling approval and saying, "Well done!" and sometimes giving me strict encouragement, his voice thundering, "Try harder!"

Day after day, I sternly reminded myself: "Buddhism is about winning, so defeat is unacceptable. If I fail, Mr. Toda's vision for kosen-rufu will suffer a setback. I must not be defeated. I must be able to report victory to him." That firmly focused prayer in my heart became a source of strength and wisdom. My bold and vigorous efforts to fulfill my vow opened the way forward and set in motion the protective functions of the universe.

My sole wish was to make Mr. Toda happy—that unwavering pledge kept me striving tirelessly, year after year.

Forward! Forward! Forward!

Victory! Victory! Victory!

I exerted myself fully as a true and devoted disciple and will, therefore, never have a single regret.

Through the shared struggle of mentor and disciple, the Soka Gakkai surmounted and triumphed over every obstacle, and finally, in December 1957, achieved the membership goal of 750,000 households. Mr. Toda's great vow was fulfilled to the letter.

The mentor's challenge is the disciple's challenge. The disciple's victory is the mentor's victory. The brilliant achievements of mentor and disciple endure for all time. The way of mentor and disciple—in particular, prayer based on the spirit of the oneness of mentor and disciple—is the heart of Nichiren Buddhism.

The Daishonin writes, "If lay believers and their teacher pray with differing minds, their prayers will be as futile as trying to kindle a fire on water" (WND-1, 795). He declares that unless our hearts are united with our mentor, our prayers will not be fulfilled. By contrast, if the prayers of mentor and disciple are perfectly aligned, they will definitely come to be realized and even make the impossible possible.

This is the formula of Nichiren Buddhism.

—*The Wisdom for Creating Happiness and Peace*, Part 3: *Kosen-rufu and World Peace* (Santa Monica, CA: World Tribune Press, 2020), 236–39.

An Ode to My Mentor, Josei Toda

O!
Then finally it arrived,
the day of Mr. Toda's inauguration as second president—
May 3, 1951,
bathed in glorious sunshine!
The mentor's triumph was
the disciple's greatest joy.

Mr. Toda declared
his resolve to accomplish
a membership of 750,000 households.
Realizing that goal
became the burning vow of my youth.

A mentor's expectations
for his true disciple
are great indeed.
And so, with the tough love
of a lion teaching its cub to survive,
Mr. Toda trained me rigorously, with strict compassion,
day after day.

My mentor
was engaged in his struggle
twenty-four hours a day.

On countless occasions,
he called me to his home
in the middle of the night,
and I always flew there
as swift as a falcon.

After summoning me to his side,
we would hold planning sessions
for our movement's future success,
just the two of us,
in the spirit of working to "assure
victory a thousand miles away."*
He charged me with
the most challenging assignments.
"If you are my disciple,
you will win!
I expect success!"
There was never a word
of praise or thanks for my efforts,
because the mark of a true disciple
is to triumph in every struggle.

I strove tirelessly, giving my all,
fighting with wholehearted devotion.
In Kamata, Bunkyo, and Sapporo,
in Osaka, Yamaguchi, and Yubari.
Wherever I went,
I raised victory banners
in unprecedented numbers

---

*See *The Writings of Nichiren Daishonin*, vol. 2 (Tokyo: Soka Gakkai, 1999), 391.

and made fresh breakthroughs
for kosen-rufu.

My mentor said
to a close circle of top leaders:
"Every place where Daisaku has been
is realizing tremendous growth
and achieving great victory.
Look at that actual proof!"

When you advance together
with your mentor,
your life burns
with passion and energy!
When you think
of your mentor,
you feel brave,
you feel strong,
and you can tap
wisdom without end!

—Excerpted from the poem
"The Song of the Unity of Mentor and Disciple,"
in *Seikyo Shimbun*, February 6, 2007.

KAMATA CAMPAIGN

◆ ◆ ◆ ◆ ◆

February 1952

Introduction

◆ ◆ ◆ ◆ ◆

THE SOKA GAKKAI [had begun] to advance toward realizing President Toda's vision of 750,000 households. But progress was slow and it didn't seem that the goal would be achieved. Toda decided to appoint the twenty-four-year-old Shin'ichi Yamamoto as an advisor to Tokyo's Kamata Chapter and have him lead propagation efforts in Kamata (in January 1952).

"My role as a disciple is to realize my mentor's aims no matter what. I will make sure that Mr. Toda's goal is attained!" thought Shin'ichi. As a youthful champion, he rose eagerly to the challenge. And in February 1952, under Shin'ichi's leadership, Kamata

Chapter welcomed an unprecedented 201 new households within a single month. This feat electrified the entire membership: "If this can be done in Kamata, we can do it too!" Everyone made a fresh determination, and a tremendous breakthrough in the kosen-rufu movement was achieved.

—"Citadel of the People" chapter, NHR-17, 222–23.

The Campaign

◆ ◆ ◆ ◆ ◆

THE DISCIPLE TAKES RESPONSIBILITY FOR HIS MENTOR'S GOAL

SHIN'ICHI HAD GROWN deeply aware of [his] profound bond with his mentor when he took on the first real battle that Toda had ever directly entrusted to him, in February 1952. He had been appointed a staff member of Kamata Chapter and had taken leadership in directing the chapter's propagation efforts.

At the chapter kickoff following his appointment, Shin'ichi frankly shared his sentiments, calling to the members: "February is the month of the Daishonin's birth, and February 11 is the day President Toda was born.

"While it goes without saying that it's because of the Daishonin's appearance in this world we could encounter this Buddhism, we also owe much to President Toda's courageous, solitary struggle for kosen-rufu. We have all received great benefit and become happy.

"To show our gratitude, let's celebrate the month of President Toda's birthday and answer his expectations by thoroughly challenging ourselves and achieving a truly magnificent victory in our activities."

As Shin'ichi pondered how, as a disciple, he could celebrate Toda's fifty-second birthday, he resolved to initiate a fresh surge of momentum for kosen-rufu.

Never for a moment did Shin'ichi forget the pledge Josei Toda had made at his inauguration as second president on May 3, 1951—a pledge to achieve a membership of 750,000 households. In fact, Shin'ichi had made it his personal goal in life as well. But the pace of the Gakkai's propagation efforts in 1952 was far too slow to actualize Toda's vision. Even the largest chapters grew up to around a hundred households at the very most each month.

"At this rate," Shin'ichi thought, "President Toda's declaration will end up a hollow promise."

He was deeply concerned and troubled by this. All his time and energy were consumed with trying to rebuild Toda's still shaky company, however. Then, one day, while he was still grappling with these problems, Toda instructed him to oversee the activities of Kamata Chapter as a chapter staff.

Shin'ichi did not want to let Toda's goal remain unfulfilled. Indeed, he was absolutely determined that this should not happen.

Fighting spirit and energy welled up inside him with the profound resolve to take personal responsibility—as Toda's disciple and on his mentor's behalf—to see that a membership of 750,000 households was realized.

As the members of Kamata Chapter listened to Shin'ichi's words at the kickoff, they became aware of his devotion and commitment to Josei Toda; they learned the true spirit of a disciple. Shin'ichi had narrowed the gap between them and Toda. They now felt much closer to their mentor in spirit. Courage and a sense of mission to work with Toda for kosen-rufu was activated deep within them.

When disciples have a seeking spirit toward their mentor and determine to fight alongside him, then the mentor's life—the mentor's commitment to kosen-rufu—pulses and flows through the disciples' veins.

Filled with a deep sense of pride and the spirit to challenge, the Kamata Chapter members joyously dedicated themselves to their activities.

—"Light of Peace" chapter, NHR-3, 289–91.

MAKING THE UNIT THE FOCUS OF ALL ACTIVITIES

[As the chapter advisor, Shin'ichi] focused entirely on the unit level, the front line of the organization. Propagation goals were set and discussion meetings held by unit. The campaign proceeded by clarifying the daily activities of each member in the unit and mutually reconfirming their determination.

Shin'ichi visited the units and encouraged the members. He spoke one to one, in small groups. He also made wholehearted effort to talk with members who didn't have a firm

self-awareness of belonging to the Soka Gakkai yet. It was solid grassroots-oriented work that went largely unseen. None of it was attention-grabbing or in the spotlight. However, it was through these efforts that members awakened to their mission and stood up to trigger a new wave of expansion.

—"Humanistic Education" chapter, NHR-24, 185.

"WE CAN DO IT IF WE TRY!"

In February, the membership grew by an unprecedented 201 households.

"We can do it if we try!"

In the midst of their great joy, everyone became keenly aware of this truth.

This stunning achievement by Kamata Chapter became an inspiration for the rest of the country, opening the way for the accomplishment of Toda's goal of 750,000 households. This struggle waged by Shin'ichi in Kamata Chapter is also the origin of the "February tradition," signifying a great leap forward in the propagation of the Daishonin's teachings.

—"Light of Peace" chapter, NHR-3, 291–92.

Recollections
Achieving the Impossible
◆ ◆ ◆ ◆ ◆

EVERYTHING BEGINS WITH PRAYER

BACK IN THOSE days, everyone just accepted as fact that one hundred was the maximum number of new members a single chapter could possibly hope to introduce in a month.

During the Kamata Campaign, however, rather than setting a chapter target, we concentrated our attention on each individual unit (today's block or group) and set a goal of two households per unit. I also offered the following three concrete guidelines: (1) Let's start with chanting daimoku,* (2) Let's treasure our neighbors, and (3) Let's share our experiences in faith.

I had practiced all three of these guidelines myself. I helped overcome the crisis faced by Mr. Toda's businesses by "praying as earnestly as though to produce fire from damp wood, or to obtain water from parched ground" (WND-1, 444). I had also always cheerfully greeted my fellow residents of the Aoba Apartments in Omori, in Tokyo's Ota Ward, and spoken to them about Buddhism whenever I had the chance. I even fondly remember doing gongyo with such neighborhood friends in my tiny apartment. In addi-

---

*daimoku: The practice of chanting Nam-myoho-renge-kyo with belief in the fundamental Law of the universe expounded by Nichiren.

tion, I had spoken to many people about my personal experience of overcoming illness through my Buddhist practice.

The members responded to and came to share my passionate determination to achieve a result that Mr. Toda would applaud.

"It's not up to others. It's up to us. We have to act now, not sometime in the future. It's not impossible! We can make it happen!"—gradually and very naturally, the hearts of the Kamata members became aligned with Mr. Toda's great vow for kosenrufu, and everyone began to take action as disciples who shared the same commitment as their mentor. . . .

By engaging in our propagation efforts with this spirit, we, the members of Kamata Chapter, not only easily broke through the upper monthly limit of one hundred households but also broke through the two hundred mark.

—"The February Campaign of the New Age,"
in *World Tribune*, April 6, 2012, 4.

THE FIRST STEP IS SETTING CLEAR GOALS

I recall the kickoff held at a local community hall in Unoki, Ota Ward, just after my new leadership appointment in Kamata Chapter. There we pledged to advance like a mighty wave. First of all, I proposed to the frontline leaders that we set a concrete goal: to increase our membership by two new households per unit during the month of February.

The first step in any challenge is to set clear goals. If the goals are vague, people will find them difficult to relate to and take on as a personal challenge. Consequently, they won't make serious efforts to realize those goals.

At the same time, it is important not to impose goals on others. Goals must be presented in such a way that everyone can accept them and be enthusiastic about realizing them. To that end, the central figure must have the firm resolve to take personal responsibility to achieve the intended target, even if he or she has to do it alone. The passion and enthusiasm emanating from such leaders inspires others to give their all for kosen-rufu.

We had just reorganized the Soka Gakkai into chapters, districts, groups, and units, in descending order of size. The unit was at the very front line of the organization, corresponding to what we in Japan now call the block level. Mr. Toda wanted to give the frontline leaders confidence and a sense of personal responsibility; and I, too, was convinced that this was crucial for the Soka Gakkai's development.

I wanted the nearly one hundred unit leaders in Kamata Chapter to take the starring roles and to be victorious. Instead of one person advancing a hundred steps, a hundred people would advance one step forward. I prayed earnestly and worked tirelessly within the chapter, determined that not even one unit would fall to the wayside, and that each member would experience benefit in faith.

The key to victory lies in uncovering fresh talent within the organization and pooling their abilities. The word *organization* tends to bring to mind an image of a monolithic and impersonal structure. However, in the Soka Gakkai, people are valued first and foremost.

All the leaders in Kamata Chapter—including group and district leaders—participated in unit-level activities. Discussion meetings were also held at the unit level because this allowed for warmer and more personal encounters. In these smaller settings, it was possible to properly address individual problems and concerns through one-to-one dialogue.

Each person who was inspired with fresh resolve at these unit-level meetings rose up courageously to propagate the Law.

Merely ordering people about will not inspire them to action. This is even more so considering that people are emotional beings.

If people feel put-upon and act only out of a sense of obligation, they are not going to display their true power.

When I took on my leadership responsibilities in Kamata, I was only twenty-four years old. How was I going to inspire everyone to take action with genuine enthusiasm and purpose? I would do it through my own actions, through my own sweat and hard work, and through producing actual results. I had resolved to take full responsibility for reaching our goal. I felt sure that if I became a good example, the members would be able to appreciate my efforts and place their trust in me.

I stood up resolutely, as befitting a youth and a disciple of Mr. Toda, and exerted myself wholeheartedly: "Watch me! Just watch my actions!" The Daishonin writes, "You need not seek far for an example" (WND-1, 614). It is our own example of personal struggle—not somebody else's—that produces sympathy and understanding in those around us.

As a chapter advisor, I worked closely together with Kamata Chapter leader Takashi Koizumi toward realizing Mr. Toda's vision. The position of chapter advisor was a support role, much like that of a vice leadership position. In that capacity, it was my function to assist the chapter leader, based on the same shared ideals and objectives.

I strove with the spirit "I will support the chapter leader so that we become the best chapter in Japan!" I made every effort to forge myself into a model chapter advisor. . . .

A month later, the results from our February Campaign were presented. Kamata Chapter came in at number one, with 201 new households! Up until that time, most chapters were unable to achieve even a hundred new households in a month. We had totally broken through that barrier and created a tremendous victory. We had achieved our unprecedented goal of introducing two new households per unit. Everyone was astonished.

No matter how difficult or painful the challenges along the way, once the goal is achieved, everything is transformed into joy and satisfaction.

Everyone was radiant with happiness and delight. Some unit leaders literally danced for joy. Nothing could have made me happier.

—From "Leadership for Kosen-rufu," in *Kosen-rufu, Our Mission*, vol. 1 (New Delhi, India: Eternal Ganges Press, 2006), 155–58.

Lessons
Inspired by the Mentor
◆ ◆ ◆ ◆ ◆

ENCOURAGING THE PERSON IN FRONT OF ME

How was I able to lead the members to victory in the February Campaign sixty years ago? It was ultimately because I did my utmost to wholeheartedly encourage the person right in front of me. . . .

All our members are noble, capable individuals who shine like sparkling diamonds. Every one of them has a mission to demonstrate the greatness of Nichiren Buddhism. They are precious and valuable without compare.

For that reason, I was eager to encourage all those who were exerting themselves tirelessly on the front lines of our movement during the February Campaign in 1952. I earnestly chanted for everyone to be able to joyfully engage in the campaign and tried to come up with all kinds of ways to inspire them so that they could freely display their full potential.

I was the youngest among the Kamata Chapter leaders at the time. If I had called meetings and acted self-importantly, who would have listened to me? My only option was to do the actual work myself, going out and personally meeting people and walking alongside the members in the cold winter wind.

I threw myself wholeheartedly into every discussion meeting I attended, every home visit I made, every letter of encouragement I wrote. I regarded each activity as if it were a decisive battleground.

When someone was having trouble sharing Buddhism with others, I took them with me when I spoke to others about our Buddhist practice, hoping they would learn from my example. And instead of doing all the talking myself, I would ask other members present to relate their personal experiences in faith or explain the basics of Buddhism to the person we were talking to. This enabled everyone to develop confidence and deepen their conviction.

Members who were older than me also stood up to take action alongside me. As a young man, I was especially heartened and gratified when men in their forties enthusiastically joined me in taking our campaign forward.

All the Kamata members actively exerted themselves to share Nichiren Buddhism with others, even though they each had personal problems of their own. It is such courage that inspires others to summon forth the strength and vitality to also stand up and bravely overcome their problems.

No one could sit still; everyone was spurred to take action. Even members who had never before spoken about their Buddhist practice to those around them, and newer members who hadn't felt confident enough to talk to others, were able to take a courageous step forward.

The unity born from valuing each individual could rightly be called the driving force for victory in the February Campaign. As the Daishonin writes, "Although Nichiren and his followers are few, because they are different in body, but united in mind [i.e., many in body, one in mind], they will definitely accomplish their great mission of widely propagating the Lotus Sutra [Nam-myoho-renge-kyo]" (WND-1, 618).

To lead the way forward, I took untold pains so that everyone could demonstrate their unique abilities and work together in unity and mutual respect. In particular, I encouraged the youth to have older members with solid, real-life experiences of the power of faith in the Mystic Law to assist them in their efforts to share Buddhism with others. The Kamata members all worked together as a team. When they heard of someone who was struggling, they went to talk to them about Buddhism. Discussion meetings were also held on an almost daily basis, seeking to relieve people of suffering and impart joy.

On one occasion, a women's division member who had just started practicing summoned up courage to visit a friend to tell her about Nichiren Buddhism, and I accompanied her. She was so nervous and anxious on the way there that her knees were shaking. I said, "Let's sing a Gakkai song and enjoy ourselves!" At first, she sang in a small, tremulous voice, but as we sang "Song of Comrades" together several times, she visibly brightened and became more positive. Although she was unable to persuade her friend to join the Soka Gakkai that day, encouraged by that experience, that same member later went on to successfully introduce many people to the practice of Nichiren Buddhism.

A whirlwind of joy swept through Kamata Chapter, as everyone continued to reach out in dialogue to one friend after another, sowing the seeds of Buddhahood by "letting people hear the teaching." We lost all track of numbers, but we must have spoken to several hundred.

By the end of February, having fought our hardest, we achieved the unprecedented monthly propagation result of 201 new households. Everyone had achieved a personal breakthrough. It was a case of new members bringing forth fresh energy and their fresh unity powering a new wave of development. . . .

There was one women's division member who worked very hard to share Buddhism with others, despite difficult personal circumstances. Even though her husband opposed her practice and she had to work on piece work at home in the evenings to augment her family's income, each morning she would set out with a couple of rice balls for her lunch and dinner and talk to others about Buddhism. Even when her efforts did not produce the results she had hoped, she continued to forge ahead unperturbed. She and her fellow members cheered each other on, engraving in their hearts the Daishonin's words "Still I am not discouraged" (WND-1, 748).

With the spirit she learned during the February Campaign—chanting and fighting with the determination to succeed without fail rather than giving up before even starting—this women's division member eventually went on to introduce more than three hundred households to the practice of Nichiren Buddhism. I am happy to say that she remains vibrantly active today, at the age of ninety-two. . . .

Nichiren Daishonin gave a lecture on his treatise "On Establishing the Correct Teaching for the Peace of the Land" at the Ikegami residence in Ota Ward shortly before his death. Mr. Toda was lecturing on this same writing when I first met him at a discussion meeting in Kamata, Ota Ward. Similarly, it was from Ota, a place of such profound and wondrous connections, that, sixty years ago, the February Campaign, through the power of ordinary people, created a movement of dialogue and solidarity for peace and happiness based on the ideals and principles of Nichiren Buddhism.

—"The February Campaign of the New Age,"
in *World Tribune*, April 13, 2012, 5 and 8.

BUNKYO CHAPTER CAMPAIGN

* * * * * *

April 1953

Introduction

◆ ◆ ◆ ◆ ◆ ◆

IN April [1953, Shin'ichi Yamamoto] was appointed acting chapter leader of [Tokyo's] Bunkyo Chapter. Bunkyo Chapter had hit a deadlock in its propagation efforts and was one of the lowest ranking chapters in the Soka Gakkai in that regard ("Citadel of the People" chapter, NHR-17, 229).

Through his vigorous struggle, the stagnating chapter soon rose to the nation's top position in propagation results ("Bold Struggle" chapter, NHR-23, 282).

The Campaign

◆ ◆ ◆ ◆ ◆ ◆

SHIN'ICHI VOWS THAT NOT A SINGLE PERSON WILL REMAIN UNHAPPY

In his youth, during the Soka Gakkai's pioneering days, Shin'ichi took the lead for kosen-rufu as acting chapter leader of Tokyo's Bunkyo Chapter. At that time, he vowed to help each and every member of the chapter become happy. He took action infused with the prayer that everyone would develop a solid daily practice, engage cheerfully in Gakkai activities, experience the great joy of sharing Buddhism with others, and gain profound conviction in faith.

Shin'ichi had always viewed becoming a leader in the Soka Gakkai as taking on the role of caring for the Buddha's disciples on behalf of the Buddha—being entrusted with the welfare of each member's life, which was more precious than the entire world. That was why he could not stand by and allow even a single individual to remain in a state of suffering and unhappiness.

Society is filled with constant challenges and change. It is difficult to safely navigate our way without strong life force, unshakable belief, and abundant wisdom—the supreme source of which is faith in the Mystic Law.

Shin'ichi chanted intently each day for the happiness of his fellow members. He personally spearheaded efforts to introduce others to Buddhism, setting an example of advancing kosen-rufu through compassionately spreading the Mystic Law. By doing so, he was also showing members the direct path to happiness.

Nichiren Daishonin writes, "The Lotus Sutra [Nam-myoho-renge-kyo] offers a secret means for leading all living beings to Buddhahood" (WND-1, 512).

Our Buddhist practice, our efforts to share Buddhism with

others, and the actualization of kosen-rufu are all for the purpose of our own happiness. Shin'ichi wanted his fellow members to know this above all and also show actual proof of becoming happy.

After Shin'ichi became acting chapter leader, the atmosphere of Bunkyo Chapter changed dramatically. From then on, discussion meetings were always filled with bright, smiling faces. This was because, quickly recognizing that the key to becoming happy lay in participating in Gakkai activities, the members actively went out and shared the Daishonin's teachings with others. And, because of this, one member after another started experiencing great benefit through their Buddhist practice.

At discussion meetings, they all eagerly vied with one another to share their experiences. Their stories struck a chord in many others' hearts, serving to encourage fellow members and also inspire their friends to begin practicing. The experiences thereby set in motion a groundswell of joyous activity.

A solid organization, an invincible organization in the realm of kosen-rufu, is one where experiences of benefit blossom endlessly in the members' lives.

—"Banner of the Law" chapter, NHR-26, 101–3.

Recollections
Achieving the Impossible

♦ ♦ ♦ ♦ ♦ ♦

THE BUNKYO CONNECTION IN THE LIVES OF TODA AND MAKIGUCHI

It was July 6, 1945. The climb up the hilly street in what is now Nishikata in Tokyo's Bunkyo Ward was painful and exhausting for our mentor, Josei Toda. It was only three days after his release from prison. Mr. Toda was on his way to confer with a friend living in Bunkyo about restoring his businesses—the first step to building a new foundation for the Soka Gakkai, which had been almost completely destroyed by the repressive policies of Japan's wartime militarist government.

His two years in prison had seriously impaired his health and sapped his strength. The summer suit he wore hung loosely on his tall, thin frame. But his eyes were fixed firmly on the future and burned with fierce determination.

It would be fair to say that Bunkyo was the place from which Mr. Toda launched his great, lifelong struggle for kosen-rufu.

Indeed, not only Josei Toda but also Tsunesaburo Makiguchi, the Soka Gakkai's founder, had a connection to Bunkyo Ward.

Mr. Makiguchi regularly visited the home of the famous educator and writer Nitobe Inazo in Kohinata, Bunkyo Ward, in order to attend meetings of the Kyodo-kai, a study and research group on the subject of Japanese regional and folk culture.

Exactly a hundred years ago (in 1903), when Mr. Makiguchi published his landmark work *A Geography of Human Life* at the age of thirty-two, he was residing in Bunkyo's Komagome area. This epic volume was completed after many indescribable challenges and hardships while living with his family in cramped rented quarters there.

Bunkyo thus can claim profound ties with both our first and second presidents.

It was fifty years ago, in April 1953, that I was appointed acting chapter leader of Bunkyo Chapter and threw myself headlong into creating a fresh groundswell for kosen-rufu there.

Bunkyo was one of the twelve original Soka Gakkai chapters, but at that time its growth had begun to stagnate and there was a discernible absence of joy and enthusiasm in the members' faith. The chapter leader was extremely concerned, and she tearfully explained the distressing situation in Bunkyo to Mr. Toda.

He was always one to take swift action. "I will dispatch my right-hand man," he said, and immediately appointed me acting chapter leader.

No one must fall by the wayside in the long journey of kosen-rufu. We must all climb the summit of victory together. For that reason, too, it is crucial that we encourage those who are facing the most painful struggles, those in regions where the situation is the most challenging.

On that unforgettable night in April 1953, I turned off Shino-bazu Avenue onto a side street and, wandering through winding, narrow alleyways, paid a visit to the chapter leader's very old, almost ramshackle home. I remember with nostalgia how hard it was to find.

My "Bunkyo revolution" started the moment I walked into that room where the leaders of the Bunkyo Chapter had gathered. When I led them in chanting three times, the members' voices weren't in unison. This was a sign that they weren't united in their struggle for kosen-rufu either. I repeated the chanting of three daimoku again and again until they could do it in unison.

Chanting is not just some empty formality. Daimoku is the most important weapon of spiritual champions, the most powerful weapon in all the universe. When we chant in unity with a common purpose, we can create an invincible alliance dedicated to the cause of good and justice. Distracted chanting is like a camera lens that is out of focus. When members' minds are not united, they are unable to summon their full strength or produce positive results.

True unity is not achieved by self-sacrifice that demands that we suppress and kill our own individuality; rather, it is attained by the expansion of our inner state of life, breaking out of the tiny shell of our lesser ego. It is a struggle in which we unite in purpose toward a lofty goal, while each of us strives to make the most of our unique talents and abilities. That is why faith based on the principle of many in body, one in mind leads to development, victory, and happiness.

More than anything, I wanted our Bunkyo members to have self-confidence. I reminded them that we were engaged in realizing kosen-rufu, a momentous endeavor beyond the abilities of the most powerful political leader, the richest tycoon. There could be no greater source of pride or glory than this.

Just because the Bunkyo members were unable to introduce Buddhism to as many people as they wished, there was no reason for them to become dispirited or depressed. They were all Bodhisattvas of the Earth. They were worthy champions of kosen-rufu who had gathered here with a mission from the beginningless past.

Stand tall, my friends! Fight on, with no regrets!

At our first meeting, I suggested an unprecedented goal. "We can do it! You haven't tried your hardest yet. Besides, you have the Gohonzon. United in our struggle under President Toda's leadership, there is nothing we cannot accomplish!"

It was not that the members were incapable. The problem was negativity and failure to use the capability they possessed.

For example, the human brain, in the cerebral cortex alone, is said to have some fourteen billion nerve cells, or neurons. Its potential is unlimited. But we usually employ only a tiny portion of that potential—some scientists suggest less than 10 percent.

Life itself is an untapped treasure trove.

If each member truly awakened to his or her mission and stood up resolutely, a sense of gratitude and joy would well forth in his or her life along with an inexhaustible fighting spirit. My role in seeing that this took place was to offer sincere encouragement and inspiration to our Bunkyo members.

I traveled to each area of Bunkyo Chapter. I wanted to do everything I could to encourage my fellow members there, with whom I had deep ties. Each one was a precious person for kosen-rufu. Each one had a profound mission. I wanted each of them without exception to stand up as a great champion of kosen-rufu.

At times I would place my hands on the shoulders of a young man and say in a way to shake his very being: "Let's work together! Let's win in life and raise a cheer at our success!" And at other times I would say to a women's division member, "Please become a victor for your family's sake and help them all lead happy lives."

—"Bunkyo: An Arena of My Youthful Struggles,"
in *Kosen-rufu, Our Mission*, vol. 2 (New Delhi, India:
Eternal Ganges Press, 2006), 65–71.

ADVANCING LIMITLESSLY WITH
THE MOTTO *"Forward!"*

At the first meeting of the chapter's group leaders, I said: "Life means moving forward; it means advancing limitlessly. Forward! was the champion Napoleon's motto. We are the champions of kosen-rufu, the champions of the struggle to refute the erroneous and reveal the true. Let us of Bunkyo Chapter burn with this spirit of advance and make Forward! our motto too!" And that's how Bunkyo's tremendous development began.

I set forth concrete goals and visited each district of the chapter, carrying out sincere one-to-one dialogues. By December of that year, Bunkyo had risen to one of the top-ranked chapters in Japan.

—"The Future Is Found in Youth," in *World Tribune*,
May 12, 2006, 2.

BECOMING HEROES WHO ILLUMINATE OTHERS
WITH THE LIGHT OF JOY

Nameless ordinary citizens helping others—nothing is more wonderful than this.

Many people have succumbed to apathy and hopelessness in these dark times in which we live. How admirable is the sight of nameless heroes plunging into society's midst and striving to turn people's hearts in the direction of happiness and joy—far more admirable than the splashy but essentially empty displays of many celebrities.

Victory or defeat in life is determined at the final moment. In life's final chapter, the verdict is strictly delivered. People of faith who have unequalled pride in their profound mission are certain to complete their lives in brilliant triumph.

My friends, never grow cowardly and seek to escape reality. For all that will remain is eternal regret. Please let the splendor of your lives, the light of your life's struggles, shine forth amid the raging waves of society.

My friends, do not fall prey to fear and become a prisoner of misfortune. Become happy! Become victors! Become nameless heroes who illuminate all around them with the light of joy!

Even when a new day dawns, society with its harsh realities remains dark. Life is about triumphing amid that bleak, merciless gloom.

No matter how dark the depths of your karma may seem at times, use the power of profound faith to overcome your weakheartedness and summon forth your courage. It is vital that you win, that you fight on bravely to surmount all obstacles, cherishing bright hope in your heart.

Toss baseless criticisms to the wayside. Ignore jealous rumors and move on. This is the way of a true champion.

Bunkyo Chapter was reborn as a beautiful Bunkyo family and a Bunkyo alliance for truth and justice, and it went on to establish a record among our chapters for introducing maximum numbers of new members—a golden achievement in the history of the Soka Gakkai that shines even more brightly today.

—"Bunkyo: An Arena of My Youthful Struggles,"
in *Kosen-rufu, Our Mission*, vol. 2 (New Delhi, India:
Eternal Ganges Press, 2011), 71–72.

Lessons
Inspired by the Mentor

◆ ◆ ◆ ◆ ◆ ◆

PRAYER IS A BURNING INNER FLAME
TO BE VICTORIOUS

Prayer to the Gohonzon, chanting daimoku, is not abstract or theoretical. It is a burning inner flame to be victorious. If that flame of resolve blazes in our heart, the instant we chant, we have already won. It is, as the Daishonin declares, like "a lantern lighting up a place that has been dark for a hundred, a thousand, or ten thousand years" (WND-1, 923). This is the practice of human revolution that is accessible to all.

Setting goals and moving forward with fresh determination . . . are the present causes that will bring splendid future results.

In April 1953, Mr. Toda asked me to take the lead in revitalizing Tokyo's Bunkyo Chapter, which had been stagnating in terms of growth. At my first meeting with the chapter, we all sat down together and chanted. In the beginning, our voices wouldn't harmonize, but as we continued to chant, everyone became more serious and our voices eventually merged into one. In this way, we were able to make a fresh, resounding start together. This change in attitude of the members led to a revolution in Bunkyo Chapter that astonished other chapters throughout Japan.

When we determine to give our all and to win in our goals and endeavors for kosen-rufu, that resolve becomes the cause for expanding our life state and bringing forth the power to achieve the impossible. It is because of such intense determination and drive that I, too, have won in every challenge I have taken on.

—"Prayer: A Cause for Victory,"
in *World Tribune*, May 15, 2009, 5.

SAPPORO SUMMER
CAMPAIGN

◆ ◆ ◆ ◆ ◆

August 1955

Introduction

❖ ❖ ❖ ❖ ❖

In August 1955, [a] summer guidance session was held in Sapporo, to which a group of leaders headed by Shin'ichi was sent from the Soka Gakkai Headquarters. During this time, Sapporo took the lead in the propagation effort that was underway in forty-five places nationwide, attaining a membership record of 388 new households. This became known as the Sapporo Summer Campaign and is remembered as a brilliant achievement in the history of the kosen-rufu movement.

—"Revitalization" chapter, NHR-15, 61.

The Campaign

◆ ◆ ◆ ◆ ◆

THE SECRET TO SUCCESS

The campaign took place over a mere ten days, and the leaders sent to Hokkaido were no more capable or trained than anyone else. So what was the secret to their success? Shin'ichi certainly didn't do anything special. But from the end of June, when he learned that he would be leading the group from Tokyo, he had made painstaking and thorough advance preparations, laying the groundwork to achieve victory in that limited period of time.

He wrote several letters to Yuai Odaka, the Sapporo Group leader, and coordinated carefully with him. The correspondence covered every detail of the movement, including the goal of introducing three hundred new households and such issues as lodging for the leaders from Tokyo, the overall itinerary, President Toda's schedule, arrangements for the place and time of the general meeting to be held there, and promoting dialogue in the activities leading up to the campaign. Shin'ichi additionally sent warm words of encouragement.

Shin'ichi's letters were shared with all the Sapporo Group members, who took steps in advance to carry out everything just as he indicated. Shin'ichi also recommended that Sapporo be divided into five districts—east, west, north, south, and central—and assigned leaders from Tokyo to work with each area. A detailed schedule was drawn up, clearly indicating when and where discussion meetings would take place. As the actual activity approached, every possible measure had been planned and taken.

Shin'ichi exerted himself with the determination that each day was crucial to making the summer guidance session a success.

If proper steps aren't taken at each moment, it will show in the outcome later. A great victory cannot be achieved without the accumulation of smaller victories.

Shin'ichi dedicated himself wholeheartedly to the task, all the while sternly reflecting on his actions and asking himself: "Did I waste any time today? Am I being slack? Do I have any regrets or second thoughts?"

Ten years Shin'ichi's senior, thirty-seven-year-old Yuai Odaka sincerely strove in preparation for the guidance trip. Just after eleven in the morning on August 16, the leaders from Tokyo arrived in Sapporo by train. Odaka, his wife, Tamiko, and other members met them at the station. Shaking Odaka's hand, Shin'ichi declared, "Mr. Odaka, we have won!" Odaka's gentle eyes sparkled with joy.

Odaka ran a water sanitation company. His business was not doing very well, however, and so, after exhausting all his options, he had joined the Soka Gakkai with his entire family two years earlier. Determined to overcome their difficulties the family gave their all to Soka Gakkai activities. Odaka was particularly resolved to use the ten days of the guidance tour to thoroughly learn about faith from Shin'ichi and construct a strong foundation on which to build the rest of his life. Not only had Odaka suffered various hardships in life, including financial difficulties, but so had many of the Sapporo members as well as the team arriving from Tokyo. Virtually none of them enjoyed financial stability.

For that reason, out of a desire to realize kosen-rufu and with an earnest prayer to do their human revolution and overcome their sufferings, each of them participated in the summer campaign. They threw themselves wholeheartedly into the campaign, and the benefits they received from their dedicated efforts were conspicuous. Everyone felt the profound joy of practicing Nichiren Buddhism and as a result deepened their conviction in faith.

Shin'ichi and the others from Tokyo conducted their activities from a modest inn located to the south of Odori Park, which runs east and west through the center of Sapporo. The morning sutra recitation took place at six each day, followed by a lecture by Shin'ichi, who covered such writings as "The Heritage of the Ultimate Law of Life," "Reply to Kyo'o," and "Reply to Ueno." Though most of the Sapporo members had joined the Soka Gakkai only less than a year earlier, they could easily understand Shin'ichi's clear lectures.

Shin'ichi read a passage from "The Heritage of the Ultimate Law of Life": "It must be ties of karma from the distant past that have destined you to become my disciple at a time like this" (WND-1, 217). He then went on to say: "These words describe the deep connection between the Daishonin and his disciples who struggled alongside him. As such, it applies equally to us, who have inherited his spirit and are devoting our lives to kosen-rufu.

"That all of us were born at this time and have gathered together now to unite our efforts in this campaign is the result of deep ties forged in the past. It is no accident. We promised Nichiren in a previous existence that we would carry out kosen-rufu. And to do so, some of us volunteered to be born poor and some to lead a life of illness.

"The place and time that we chose in the past to begin our great struggle is none other than Sapporo, Hokkaido, in August 1955. You have all assembled here to participate in this great campaign so that you can change your karma of poverty or illness and demonstrate the greatness of the Mystic Law. If you are firmly aware of this, you cannot fail to exhibit tremendous ability. With the Gohonzon, we will never be deadlocked. Let us fight with zest and high spirits!"

Shin'ichi's lecture struck the members deeply. As they listened, they realized that their mission stemmed from the remote past and were thrilled to participate in this historic struggle that would determine the future of kosen-rufu. They all rose to the challenge, their excitement fueling their efforts. United in spirit, the leaders from Tokyo and the local members went out into the streets of Sapporo filled with a fresh sense of purpose.

Shin'ichi also threw himself into the struggle. He keenly felt that to achieve victory it was crucial to meet and talk with as many members as possible, encouraging and supporting them here, where they were carrying out their valiant struggles. He therefore went around participating in discussion meetings and visiting members' homes. After encouraging a member living in the suburbs, he would turn up half an hour later at a meeting place in downtown Sapporo. He moved so quickly that he seemed to be everywhere at once. It was on the back of Yuai Odaka's motor scooter that he was able to travel from place to place so speedily.

After one of Shin'ichi's morning lectures, he told a women's division member present that he would be attending her discussion meeting later that day. At the appointed time, the woman waited outside for Shin'ichi to arrive. A scooter approached, but she didn't pay much attention to it. Then she heard a voice: "Hi! Sorry to have kept you waiting!" When she turned around, Shin'ichi was standing at her side.

She had thought that Shin'ichi would surely arrive by taxi or car; it never occurred to her he would come riding on the back of a scooter. Shin'ichi explained to the astonished member: "This is the fastest way to get around. It makes it possible for me to attend more meetings." Shin'ichi didn't care about outward appearances. Victory was his only concern.

At the time, many of the back streets and alleyways in Sapporo were either unpaved or quite bumpy. Riding behind Odaka, Shin'ichi bounced up and down. At times he was jarred so badly that his back hurt. Nevertheless, determined to win in every strug-gle, he continually chanted under his breath as they went. Moreover, around this time, his health wasn't very good. His appetite was poor, and some days it was all he could do to drink water or juice.

Still, he never appeared tired. His fighting spirit only burned more ardently. If a leader gives in to exhaustion, he or she cannot inspire and invigorate others. Knowing that victory could not be realized without the strenuous efforts of his fellow members, Shin'ichi had decided in his heart that he would praise and encourage them with all his might.

When members started to feel tired or discouraged, he would lead them in singing a song, and sometimes he would sing for them. He would also perform the Japanese folk dance "Kuroda Bushi" on occasion. Shin'ichi's fierce determination overflowed in his vigorous movements, touching the hearts of all who watched. Even the dimly lit meeting place seemed to brighten. Inspired by Shin'ichi's selfless actions, both the leaders from Tokyo and the local members renewed their resolve and continued to exert themselves to the utmost.

A member who took part in the Sapporo Summer Campaign later recalled: "As the leader of our struggle, Mr. Yamamoto exhibited incredible passion and determination to win no matter what. Everyone who came into contact with him was inspired to do their very best.

"But that wasn't all. He was also sincerely concerned about every one of us. In fact, that was the real source of our energy. Whenever he met one of us, he would express his appreciation and ask about our family members. We were so touched by his devotion to us that we felt we really had to give the campaign our all."

Launched on August 16, the campaign gained momentum day by day, and on August 20, the goal of three hundred new households had already been achieved. By the final day of the campaign, 388 households had been introduced to Nichiren Buddhism, setting a brilliant national record.

—"Revitalization" chapter, NHR-15, 61–68.

Lessons
Inspired By the Mentor
◆ ◆ ◆ ◆ ◆ ◆

EVERY MEETING, EVERY HOME VISIT HAS TO BE THE BEST

In the February Campaign in Tokyo's Kamata Chapter, the summer guidance tour in Sapporo, the Osaka Campaign, and in the propagation campaign in Yamaguchi Prefecture, he had planned everything with tremendous care. He never held a single meeting that was neither focused nor exploding with joy. To do otherwise would be an insult to those who made time to attend the meeting; it would be stealing their time, he believed.

That's why he not only thought very carefully about everything he would say, but carried out detailed checks of each meeting's agenda, the speeches of the other speakers, and even the arrangement and the lighting in the room, in an effort to make every meeting the best possible. Compromise is the breeding ground of failure.

"It all comes down to renewing the spirits of the participants and filling them with great joy and a burning fighting spirit!"

He was in earnest. He made a wholehearted effort to make every meeting, every planning session, and every home visit the best possible. That's the key to victory.

—"Courage" chapter, NHR-23, 238.

KANSAI CAMPAIGN

— ◆ ◆ ◆ ◆ ◆ —

January to May 1956

Introduction

◆ ◆ ◆ ◆ ◆ ◆

I N THE EARLY days of the Soka Gakkai, the membership in Kansai was very small compared to that of Tokyo, and the organization was thus rather weak. But in January 1956, President Toda, keenly perceiving Kansai's strategic importance in his overall vision of the future of kosen-rufu movement, dispatched Shin'ichi there to take the lead in activities.

At first, the local members thought that they would never be a match for the Tokyo members. Shin'ichi, therefore, focused all his energy on transforming each person's inner resolve, calling out to them: "Let's build an indestructible golden citadel of Soka in

Kansai!" and "Let's wage a struggle for kosen-rufu that will be an example for the rest of Japan!"

Inspired by the passion of their youthful leader, the Kansai members underwent a great shift in attitude. They began to believe that they were the protagonists of kosen-rufu and that Kansai was the movement's main arena. Thus, they all stood up as champions of the cause and set out enthusiastically to share Nichiren Buddhism with others.

As a result of their efforts, Osaka Chapter increased its membership by 11,111 households in the single month of May of that year, achieving an unprecedented record that shines eternally in the annals of kosen-rufu.

—"Guiding Star" chapter, NHR-13, 126.

The Campaign

◆ ◆ ◆ ◆ ◆

JANUARY 1956 . . . WHEN THE GREAT STRUGGLE TO TRANSFORM KANSAI BEGAN

In the . . . year 1956, his mentor Josei Toda entrusted Shin'ichi with the task of building the Kansai region into a solid citadel of kosen-rufu that equaled or surpassed Tokyo. From the start of the year, Shin'ichi was dispatched to Kansai to exercise leadership in accomplishing that goal. . . .

Shin'ichi left for Osaka on January 4. He visited Kansai numerous times following that first trip.

He had to pay for his own travel expenses and other costs. It was quite difficult scraping the money together. At the same time, while taking leadership in Kansai, he was also working as sales manager for the Daito Commerce Company in Tokyo, for which

Toda was a consultant, and serving as Soka Gakkai youth division chief of staff and acting chapter leader of Tokyo's Bunkyo Chapter, among other responsibilities.

Building Kansai into an indestructible, mighty bastion was the top priority. If he failed, Toda's vision of kosen-rufu would never be realized.

When Shin'ichi thought of the heavy responsibility resting on his shoulders, he became seized with an acute sense of anxiety and lost his appetite. At the beginning of the New Year, he even came down with fever. The other leaders who were using the New Year's holiday as an excuse to relax seemed incredibly easygoing to him.

This is how the great struggle to transform Kansai began.

Shin'ichi adopted an iron-clad rule for victory: He would never even think of asking others to do what needed to be done. He would always take the initiative and create a ripple effect through his own diligent efforts.

Shin'ichi started to chant alone at the Soka Gakkai Kansai Headquarters building in Osaka. Everything starts with prayer. Observing Shin'ichi chanting so earnestly and intensely to build Kansai into a shining bastion of kosen-rufu, a few men's chapter leaders and others joined him. Gradually more and more members began to chant with him, until the Gohonzon room at the headquarters was full.

Shin'ichi also held lectures after morning gongyo. This imparted courage to the members. The joy and sense of mission as Bodhisattvas of the Earth who show their neighbors in Kansai the way to happiness began to beat vibrantly in their hearts.

Shin'ichi initiated his activities by traveling extensively throughout Osaka to encourage the members. He usually traveled on a bicycle borrowed from a local member. Sometimes he'd get a flat tire and end up walking the bicycle through the dark night streets.

To encourage members, he even visited areas where tiny houses were crammed along narrow alleyways pervaded by the smell of fish being grilled. He also went to areas where farm fields stretched out to the horizon.

Most of the members greeted him with joy, appreciative that he had made the effort to visit. Some gave him a cool reception. But Shin'ichi greeted them all with a warm smile, engaged them in dialogue, and encouraged them.

In addition, he attended numerous discussion meetings, taking action on the front lines of propagation efforts. At one particular discussion meeting in Higashi Osaka, his sincere and confident dialogue convinced seventeen of the eighteen guests in attendance to join the Soka Gakkai.

Spiritual inspiration is a force for victory. We must ignite the life force of others with our own burning life force. Witnessing Shin'ichi's valiant struggle, the Kansai leaders were deeply moved and impressed, thinking: "This is what it means to be a real leader.

When we strive with everything we've got, we can expand our life states. Let's do it!"

Shin'ichi's vibrant initiative thus inspired the entire membership and produced any number of "Shin'ichi Yamamotos" striving at his side. . . .

Shin'ichi ardently explained to the Osaka members that Josei Toda, who had stood up alone for kosen-rufu, was their mentor. And he told them of Toda's cherished vow to eliminate the suffering of all people not only in Osaka and Kansai, but also in Japan, and indeed, the entire world.

He exhorted: "Let's make President Toda's wish our own and, as his representatives, fight to make it a reality! By doing that, we can forge a direct link with this outstanding leader of kosen-rufu, President Toda. And that's a tremendous source of power for us. Thinking of Mr. Toda, you'll feel courage rise in your heart. You'll be invigorated. As you engage in your daily struggles, please keep a vision of President Toda in your mind and, while striving together, carry on an inner dialogue with him—'President Toda, just watch me!' 'What would you, President Toda, do in this case?'"

In the struggle to advance kosen-rufu, the key to unity lies in remaining in perfect harmony with the spirit of our Buddhist mentor. A bicycle wheel can turn only when all the spokes are firmly anchored to the hub. The mentor is like the wheel's hub.

With Shin'ichi's leadership, the Kansai organization began its remarkable advance. In March, the Osaka Chapter added 5,005 new households and the Sakai Chapter, 759. In April, the Osaka Chapter added 9,002 households and the Sakai Chapter, 1,111.

In May, marking the fifth anniversary of Josei Toda's inauguration as the second president of the Soka Gakkai, Osaka Chapter introduced Nichiren Buddhism to 11,111 households, and Sakai Chapter, 1,515.

The Kansai members each shared the determination of Shin'ichi Yamamoto: "President Toda is my mentor in propagation. As his disciple, I want to commemorate the anniversary of his inauguration with a major achievement in propagation."

The growth in membership of the two Kansai chapters represented 44 percent of the Soka Gakkai's total increase in membership at that time. It was a truly unprecedented achievement and an everlasting golden record. A magnificent bastion of kosen-rufu had been established in Kansai.

—"Courage" chapter, NHR-23, 204–9.

Recollections
Achieving the Impossible

◆ ◆ ◆ ◆ ◆ ◆

THE MENTOR-DISCIPLE SPIRIT BUILT
EVER-VICTORIOUS KANSAI

The members in Kansai possess the spirit of mentor and disciple. No one can ever sever the spiritual ties between me and the Kansai members, the shared commitment to fight passionately to realize kosen-rufu. Nor will we ever allow the sullied hands of authoritarian powers to touch that precious bond.

Everything begins and ends with the mentor-disciple relationship—this is the spirit that has built Ever-Victorious Kansai.

When Josei Toda became the second president of the Soka Gakkai fifty years ago [in 1951], one of the first things I said to him was: "For the future development of kosen-rufu in Japan, we should give top priority to constructing a chapter in Osaka, the capital of the people." Mr. Toda replied on the spot: "All right. If that's what you think, Daisaku, you go to Osaka and build the chapter there."

The construction of our organization in Kansai began from this unity of spirit between mentor and disciple. At the time, we had hardly any members in Osaka, and the top Soka Gakkai leaders never even dreamed of establishing a chapter there. But Mr. Toda had declared that he would achieve a membership of 750,000 households. And I was his disciple. As such, I thought long and hard, with the enthusiasm and idealism of youth, about what was necessary to realize the widespread propagation of Nichiren Buddhism. And it was this that prompted me to make my suggestion of establishing a chapter in Kansai to my mentor.

While Tokyo is Japan's political and administrative capital, Osaka—indeed, all of Kansai—is its commercial capital. If we could establish a strong base for kosen-rufu there, the ripples of its forward momentum would undoubtedly spread to other areas such as Chugoku, Shikoku, Kyushu, and eventually all of Japan.

[*In 1951, when President Toda made his declaration to achieve a membership of 750,000 households, the total membership of the Soka Gakkai was a little more than three thousand people in twelve chapters. In August 1952, there were only some forty members in Osaka.*]

The following year, 1952, the beginnings of Osaka Chapter took form. I went to Osaka on August 14 of that year, and Mr. Toda followed the next day. . . .

Mr. Toda clearly stated his purpose for going to Osaka, saying: "Let us rid Osaka of all sickness and poverty!" This was a solemn declaration to wipe the tears of unhappiness and suffering from the eyes of the people of Osaka. I made Mr. Toda's vow my own. To achieve that goal, I would have to dedicate myself earnestly to propagating the Mystic Law and imparting courage to many people so that they could lead happy lives. . . .

As a result of this determination, strong, courageous individuals, who had awakened to a new way of living and found a new social awareness, stood up to work for the reform and betterment of the society in which they lived. . . .

"We must build Osaka—a city of honest, industrious people—into a capital of happiness of the people overflowing with good-will"—this was my determination as a young lion of twenty-eight who, from the start of 1956, began to take active leadership in the construction of Ever-Victorious Kansai. Together with the Kansai members, I launched a concerted effort—a struggle of faith and kosen-rufu—to achieve that goal. . . .

I had only one mission: to build an undefeatable golden citadel in Kansai. To do so, I was determined to give my entire life and resolutely triumph. But the sheer size of the goal that President

Toda had set made it an undertaking that was physically impossible for a single individual to achieve all alone. I therefore resolved to put 100 percent effort into meeting the Kansai members, into encouraging them, spurring them on, and raising them to be courageous champions of kosen-rufu who would work with me in this struggle. And I translated this into action. I was certain that my burning determination—the passionate flame of the human spirit that could make the impossible possible beyond imagining—would definitely spread and set alight the hearts of many others.

I wanted to win. I had to win. Winning and then reporting that victory to my mentor was my supreme mission as a disciple; it was also the actual practice of the teaching of the oneness of mentor and disciple.

I chanted sincerely day after day to have the strength to achieve my goal. I chanted continuously with the firm conviction that everyone I came in contact with would become an ally of our movement or would function as a protective force.

Our propagation efforts in Osaka in 1956, which our members throughout Japan were watching expectantly, gained dynamic, explosive momentum, day by day, month by month.

The organization's overall momentum is determined by the energy and the tenacity of purpose of the leaders.

I boldly took the initiative, throwing my entire being into the struggle. I never hesitated, staying constantly on the go and speaking without rest. I spent every day, from early morning until late at night, encouraging our members in every corner of Osaka. There were times when I attended twenty-five or twenty-six meetings in a single day, always on the move, always telling myself, "I have time for one more" and "I can encourage more members." I was drenched with sweat, my voice was hoarse from speaking, and my legs felt like cement. There were so many people I had to meet, so many people I wanted to see and encourage, so many people I wanted to contact within the limited time of each twenty-four-hour day. If I let this moment, this opportunity pass by, I might never be able to see this person again. That's why I was so desperate to make the most of every second.

While traveling from one meeting place to another, if someone pointed out a member's house to me I would always try to stop by, even if just for a minute. Whenever a member came to the Kansai Headquarters, I would always try to make time to speak with him or her, even if just a word of greeting or encouragement. At times when I simply could not stop, I would wave or acknowledge people with my eyes, silently sending daimoku to them from my heart.

I knew that if our hearts touched for even a moment we could forge a connection for Buddhism; but if I just passed by without reaching out, nothing of value would be created.

Human revolution is meeting people. Kosen-rufu is talking with people. These actions embody courage, wisdom, and compassion.

Wherever I went, exciting dramas of life-to-life inspiration and communion unfolded, giving rise to expanding waves of joy.

If I stopped by the home of a local leader but they happened to be out, I always left a message of encouragement for them with their family. And as I made the rounds of the local meeting places—usually the members' homes—I would take up my writing brush and present the members with pieces of calligraphy, hoping to encourage them in any way I could. I would write words for them like "Decisive Battle," "Courageous Struggle," and "Great Triumph."

In a flash, a wave of fellow feeling spread. And a ready and responsive fighting spirit to work together for the common cause of kosen-rufu was soon established. All my trusty fellow members in Osaka grasped my aims and determinations. They rose up and exerted themselves tirelessly alongside me, sharing both joys and sufferings.

I read countless passages of Nichiren's writings with the Kansai members. Among them was: "One day of life is more valuable than all the treasures of the major world system" (WND-1, 955).

Let us do all we can on this precious, irreplaceable day that is today so that we have no regrets, and devote our lives to kosen-rufu and the happiness of humanity! Being ever-victorious means winning resolutely in the present; it means winning today.

Making their way through arduous trials in perfect accord with this spirit of the Daishonin, the members of Kansai finally triumphed! In May of that turbulent 1956, we realized the magnificent monthly record of enabling 11,111 households to receive the Gohonzon. This achievement firmly secured the foundations of the golden citadel of kosen-rufu in Kansai.

—"Osaka: Japan's Great Citadel of the People," in *Kosen-rufu,*
Our Mission, vol. 2 (New Delhi, India: Eternal Ganges Press,
2006), 73–79.

Lessons
Inspired By the Mentor

◆ ◆ ◆ ◆ ◆ ◆

LECTURES OF CONVICTION BRING FORTH
LIMITLESS COURAGE AND STRENGTH

Kansai Youth Leader: I understand that your daily morning lectures on the writings of Nichiren Daishonin at the old Kansai Headquarters during the Osaka Campaign started from eight in the morning, and members apparently attended not only from Osaka but from all over the Kansai region.

President Ikeda: Some members even took the first train in the morning to attend. Everyone was really dedicated. I was also in earnest. That's why our hearts were united and we could bring forth unlimited strength. I would pour my all into each lecture as if "exhausting the pains and trials of millions of kalpas" (see OTT, 214), constantly thinking how I could convey the great beneficial power of practicing Nichiren Buddhism to those who were still young in faith. When the lecture was over, everyone would leave the room surging with vigor.

I encouraged members based on the Daishonin's writings not just at the morning lectures but also at various other meetings and personal guidance sessions.

At the very beginning of the Osaka Campaign, I quoted the passage "I am praying that, no matter how troubled the times may become, the Lotus Sutra and the ten demon daughters will protect all of you, praying as earnestly as though to produce fire from damp wood, or to obtain water from parched ground" (WND-1, 444).

Viewed from the general opinion of society, it may have seemed like our undertaking was impossible. However, with faith and strong prayer, we could definitely make the impossible possible. I was determined to deeply instill this conviction in the hearts of our members. The Daishonin states, "Employ the strategy of the Lotus Sutra before any other" (WND-1, 1001). This was my consistent message to the members and something I personally demonstrated through my actions during the Osaka Campaign.

Kansai Youth Leader: Many pioneering Kansai members have remarked on how you tailored your guidance based on the Daishonin's writings according to the time or circumstances.

For instance, when you sensed that members weren't in rhythm with one another, you would emphasize the importance of solidarity, citing the passage "If the spirit of many in body but one in mind prevails among the people, they will achieve all their goals, whereas if one in body but different in mind, they can achieve nothing remarkable" (WND-1, 618).

And when you thought the determination of an area's central leader was faltering, you would encourage the person by quoting the passage "In battles soldiers regard the general as their soul. If the general were to lose heart, his soldiers would become cowards" (WND-1, 613).

—*Youth and the Writings of Nichiren Daishonin*
(Santa Monica, CA: World Tribune Press, 2012), 83–84.

YAMAGUCHI CAMPAIGN

October/November 1956
and January 1957

Introduction

◆ ◆ ◆ ◆ ◆ ◆

THE YAMAGUCHI CAMPAIGN [was] a large-scale propagation campaign that took place under Shin'ichi Yamamoto's leadership in October and November 1956 and January 1957, a golden achievement in the history of kosen-rufu. Members with connections to Yamaguchi had gathered from throughout Japan to take part, energetically spreading Nichiren Buddhism. The propagation efforts in 1956 and 1957 expanded membership in Yamaguchi Prefecture from about four hundred households to nearly ten times that.

—"Shared Struggle" chapter, NHR-25, 98.

The Campaign

◆ ◆ ◆ ◆ ◆ ◆

THE GREAT STRUGGLE BEGAN FROM THE SHARED COMMITMENT OF MENTOR AND DISCIPLE

Shin'ichi spoke in a friendly, informal manner.

"I took the lead in the Yamaguchi Campaign after I received direct instructions from President Toda.

"At the time, kosen-rufu in Yamaguchi was far behind that of other regions. At the start of September 1956, Mr. Toda summoned me over and asked if I'd create a turning point in the development of kosen-rufu in Yamaguchi: 'Would you like to initiate a whirlwind of guidance and propagation activities in Yamaguchi Prefecture?'

"I responded without hesitation, 'Yes! I'll take care of it.'

"That great struggle began from the shared commitment of mentor and disciple."

Shin'ichi called on members of every chapter throughout Japan who had some connection to Yamaguchi to participate in the pioneering campaign.

At that time, many Soka Gakkai members' lives were filled with hardship, but they valiantly agreed to take part in spite of it. The members who went to Yamaguchi were participants of a volunteer movement for kosen-rufu.

Many members from Kansai were eager to strive alongside Shin'ichi, then youth division chief of staff, and were willing to travel anywhere. The participants regarded dedicating their lives to kosen-rufu as the highest honor. They fully understood that it was the way to live a truly noble life.

The united purpose of Shin'ichi and his mentor, Josei Toda, and

the unity of all the members and Shin'ichi—that was what led to
the great victory achieved in the Yamaguchi Campaign.

—"Shared Struggle" chapter, NHR-25, 150–51.

STRUGGLING TO SOW THE SEEDS
OF BUDDHAHOOD

Members from twenty-six chapters throughout Japan were dispatched to Yamaguchi to take part in the Yamaguchi Campaign.
Some of them were from Sendai and other parts of Tohoku.
The chapters, actively engaging in various activities, competed
against one another to be the best at sowing the seeds of happiness
throughout Yamaguchi. . . .

Most of those dispatched to Yamaguchi were relatively new
members, who had joined only a year or two earlier. They had all
scrimped and saved to pay for their own travel, food, and lodging.

When they returned home, many still faced their own struggles
with poverty, illness of loved ones, or family discord. But they
were enthusiastic and energized, sincerely joining the campaign
out of their determination to polish their lives through the effort
to break free of their negative karma.

Even though they chose whom they would call on through various kinds of personal connections, almost no one was interested
in hearing what they had to say about Buddhism. Many became
disheartened.

Gazing at the lights of the town from a hill, some members
felt discouraged that in spite of all the people who lived there,
they hadn't been able to introduce a single one of them to this
Buddhism.

Shin'ichi, who was leading the propagation campaign, brought
the light of courage to these members and ignited a fighting spirit.
Consoling those who hadn't shown results in their propagation

efforts, he earnestly encouraged them by saying: "There are two kinds of propagation, that is, to sow the seed of Buddhahood: letting people hear the teaching and leading people to arouse faith in the teaching. The former is clear—letting people hear the teaching; the latter is leading people to arouse faith in the teaching and accept the Gohonzon.

"Even if the people you speak to don't start practicing immediately, you have planted the seeds of Buddhahood in their heart, so they will eventually accept this faith. Enabling people to hear about Buddhism is the basis of propagation."

Shin'ichi empathized with these members and urged: "We may tend to feel disappointed and dispirited if, despite how earnestly we try to share Buddhism with others, they don't take faith. But the benefits obtained through letting people hear the teaching and leading people to arouse faith in the teaching are the same. The important thing is to speak out and share the correct teachings of Buddhism.

"You all know about Bodhisattva Never Disparaging. Our prop-

agation efforts to plant the seeds of Buddhism are the modern-day equivalent of his practice. Isn't that amazing?". . .

To boldly share Buddhism with others, even with those who do not wish to hear, [is] to enable them to form a connection to Buddhism. This spirit is also demonstrated in the actions of Bodhisattva Never Disparaging.

Those who hear the teaching of the Mystic Law may not accept it immediately. They may reject it. . . . Through having heard the Law, though, a connection to Buddhism has been forged in their lives, and the seed for attaining Buddhahood has been sown within them. . . .

Shin'ichi Yamamoto said to the members participating in the Yamaguchi Campaign: "Whether a person who has heard about Buddhism chooses to accept it or not is up to them. What matters is how many people we're able to share Buddhism with, based on our genuine desire for their happiness.

"Our goal is for each person to find true happiness through

practicing Nichiren Buddhism. Therefore, it goes without saying that it's very important for you to have a strong desire that they begin practicing for themselves. But even if they don't practice Buddhism, there's no need to be disillusioned or disappointed.

"Try talking to one person. If it doesn't go well, try talking to two more people. If that still doesn't work out, try three, five, ten, and if ten are unfruitful, then try twenty. If twenty doesn't work out, then try thirty and forty. The point is just to keep sharing this Buddhism, with conviction and in high spirits. All those efforts will be transformed into benefit and good fortune, a force for transforming your karma.

"We are all 'Bodhisattvas Never Disparaging' of the modern day, the Bodhisattvas of the Earth. We're following the same great path of Buddhist practice as Nichiren Daishonin."

The members who heard Shin'ichi's guidance felt courage welling up within them. Their spirits were revived, and they set out again with a fresh determination to share Buddhism with others. . . .

At the first discussion meeting attended by Shin'ichi in Hagi [in Yamaguchi] during the campaign, Tokiko Igo, who had just recently joined the Soka Gakkai, asked with an intense expression, "Can this Buddhist practice really help me overcome my illness?"

She had joined just a month ago and was suffering from tuberculosis of the lungs and kidneys.

"What's wrong?" asked Shin'ichi.

"I have tuberculosis."

Her husband, who was sitting nearby, listened intently to their exchange. He was an employee of the Japanese National Railways. He also had a bronchial condition and was suffering from chronic coughing and phlegm. He hadn't yet joined the Soka Gakkai, but he had come to the meeting at the request of Tokiko, who wasn't fully mobile on her own.

Looking at Tokiko, Shin'ichi spoke of the connection between karma and illness.

"The power of medicine is very important, but overcoming an illness depends, in the end, on your life force. As long as you don't transform the karma of suffering from illness, you may recover from one illness but you'll only come down with another. Buddhism teaches the way to bring forth your inner life force and transform your karma. I also suffered from tuberculosis in the past, but I was able to overcome it."

When we speak with conviction based on our own personal experiences, our words have the power to profoundly move other people's hearts.

In response to Shin'ichi's words, Tokiko Igo stood up with the firm determination to transform her karma through her Buddhist practice.

Her husband, Tadaharu, also decided to begin practicing Nichiren Buddhism.

Tokiko was inspired and immediately invited three friends to a discussion meeting at the inn where Shin'ichi and the others were staying.

All three listened eagerly to Shin'ichi's words, apprehending the importance of upholding a correct philosophy, and decided to join the Soka Gakkai on the spot.

Tokiko experienced the joy of sharing this Buddhism. Hope, joy, and conviction overflowed from her heart like vibrant music.

From that time on, whenever she was feeling well enough she actively participated in Soka Gakkai activities. She found that when she exerted herself to share Buddhism with others, she forgot that she was even ill.

Without her noticing, the lethargy that had always plagued her disappeared and she was brimming with vitality.

That December she recovered from her illness, and in the following April the hematuria that she had suffered from for so long stopped. She was able to bring her eight-year struggle with illness to a successful close.

Josei Toda often said: "The Gohonzon represents the strongest concentration of the universal life force. When we connect with the Gohonzon in our lives, our life force also gains that same strength."

When we are actively striving for the kosen-rufu movement and for the sake of the happiness of others, we are filled with vibrant life force.

Observing the experience of his wife Tokiko, Tadaharu also became enthusiastic in his practice, and the two of them together became a driving force for kosen-rufu in Hagi.

—"Shared Struggle" chapter, NHR-25, 109–15.

Encouraged by Shin'ichi, Another Pioneer Member Overcomes Illness

In November 1956, Toshiko Yamamura attended a discussion meeting Shin'ichi had led in Tokuyama [in Yamaguchi Prefecture]. She had always been sickly, suffering for many years from asthma and the side effects of the many drugs she took. Her husband's business of making and selling konnyaku* products was doing poorly, and she was always struggling to make ends meet.

During the discussion meeting, Shin'ichi asked Toshiko to move to the front of the room.

She had no inclination toward religion at all. She expected to hear some kind of suspicious claims and, as she moved toward the front of the group, she was determined to oppose and argue vigorously against them.

"Do you have any worries or troubles?" asked Shin'ichi. Of course, her days were filled with all sorts of worries. Irritated at this intrusion into her personal life, she resisted.

"Not really, no."

Shin'ichi just smiled at her and began to speak in a calm manner about the importance of following a correct philosophy and explaining the basics of Buddhism.

In her heart, Toshiko found him convincing. But at the same time, she was determined not to succumb to his persuasion.

There are times when, even though one knows intellectually that something is true, one is too emotional to accept it and act on it. But the way to genuine happiness starts with controlling one's emotions and courageously taking the first step toward progress and self-improvement.

---

* Konnyaku: Also, konjac. A plant whose corms are used to produce flour and gelatinous food products.

When he'd finished his presentation, Shin'ichi said to Toshiko: "Are you sure you're not ill? The most important step for overcoming illness is to chant Nam-myoho-renge-kyo to the Gohonzon and strengthen your life force. Why don't you try practicing this Buddhism?"

She looked at Shin'ichi and asked in a sarcastic tone: "Excuse me for asking, but it seems to me that the Gohonzon is just a piece of paper. Why should mere words written on a piece of paper have such power?"

Shin'ichi responded sincerely: "Paper can have remarkable power, can't it? Would you toss away a check for fifty or a hundred thousand yen because it's 'just paper'? If you get a telegram saying, YOUR MOTHER IS IN CRITICAL CONDITION, wouldn't you still be deeply affected, even though it's just words on paper?

"A map is just paper. But if we have trust in the map and use it, we will arrive at our intended destination. The Gohonzon is the object of devotion for bringing forth a great state of life so that we can become genuinely happy."

Shin'ichi continued to give numerous other examples to make his case. . . .

Before leaving the room, he said one more time to Toshiko, "I hope you will try practicing this Buddhism and become truly happy."

Toshiko did not respond. However, she was profoundly touched by Shin'ichi's warmth, and as a result she was almost inclined to begin practicing Buddhism. But she felt that doing so would somehow be a sign of defeat.

Nevertheless, after a while, she joined the Soka Gakkai and decided to put the Gohonzon to test in order to prove Shin'ichi and the other Soka Gakkai members wrong.

She chanted earnestly for a week, then stopped the next week. The result was indisputable. From the day she started chanting, her asthma attacks stopped completely. When she ceased chanting, she suffered such a painful attack that she thought she was going to die.

"Now I understand the great power of the Gohonzon! I believe now! I want to overcome my illness!" Toshiko apologized intensely before the Gohonzon. . . .

The irrevocable proof Toshiko experienced awakened her to the power of Buddhist faith . . . [and] she exerted herself wholeheartedly in Soka Gakkai activities. . . .

In August 1964, when the Higashi Tokuyama Chapter was established, she was appointed the chapter's women's leader.

Based on pure-hearted faith, she forged an invincible spirit and determination that resulted in the dynamic expansion of kosen-rufu in Tokuyama.

—"Shared Struggle" chapter, NHR-25, 162–65.

Recollections
Achieving the Impossible

◆ ◆ ◆ ◆ ◆ ◆

A BATTLE FOR THE LAW, A HISTORIC CAMPAIGN

On September 5, 1956, I was conferring with Mr. Toda about the future of kosen-rufu. The focus of our discussion was Yamaguchi Prefecture in the Chugoku region of Japan. At the time, we had a membership of only a few more than four hundred households there. Yamaguchi was the starting point of events that led to the Meiji Restoration and Japan's subsequent modernization and had produced many of the nation's leaders. Without a doubt, it would remain an important region in Japan.

Mr. Toda said to me: "Our organization in Chugoku is lagging furthest behind. Daisaku, I want you to go there and take the lead in giving guidance in faith and creating a groundswell of propagation."

I immediately replied, "Yes, I will do my best!" This was the start of the historic Yamaguchi Campaign. I was twenty-eight at the time.

That day, I wrote in my diary: "He [Mr. Toda] indicated that next month, there will be a full-scale propagation campaign in Yamaguchi Prefecture. I will take full responsibility. . . . I will fight like [Minamoto no] Yoshitsune or [Takasuji] Shinsaku. It will be a battle for the Law that shall go down in history."

The Yamaguchi Campaign took place in three stages, in October, November, and then the following January. Members from all over Japan who had some kind of connection with Yamaguchi courageously volunteered to take part.

Nichiren Daishonin writes, "[Chanting] Nam-myoho-renge-kyo with the spirit of many in body but one in mind . . . is the basis for the universal transmission of the ultimate Law of life and death" (WND-1, 217).

The true heritage of Buddhism pulses in united efforts to advance kosen-rufu. During the Yamaguchi Campaign, I encouraged our members with this passage. Over the course of a total of twenty-two days, we expanded our membership in Yamaguchi to more than four thousand households—an almost tenfold increase.

I wrote in my diary (on January 28, 1957), "Will pour all my ability and effort into struggling to transform my destiny and lay the strategic groundwork for kosen-rufu." And as that entry indicates, I gave my all to ensure the success of the Yamaguchi Campaign. I never just made a show of taking action.

The Yamaguchi Campaign was an earnest struggle to transform the resolve of our members in Yamaguchi and achieve a fresh breakthrough for kosen-rufu. At the same time, it had a more profound and broad-ranging purpose—to secure the future of the Soka Gakkai as a whole, as well as the future of Japan.

Mr. Toda was very happy with our triumph in Yamaguchi.

—"Entrusting the Future to the Youth," at a youth division representatives conference, August 1, 2008, in *Seikyo Shimbun*, August 7, 2008.

Lessons
Inspired by the Mentor
◆ ◆ ◆ ◆ ◆

HAVING AN UNSHAKEABLE DETERMINATION TO ACHIEVE VICTORY

During [the Yamaguchi Campaign], I focused on three points. The first was to have an unshakable determination to achieve victory.

Over the course of those three months, from October to January, I traveled to Yamaguchi Prefecture three times. I spent a total of twenty-two days there leading the short but decisive struggle. On top of that, I was striving wholeheartedly to help Mr. Toda's businesses and support the Soka Gakkai overall. Every step was a battle against time. The challenge was compounded by the fact that some of the senior leaders didn't grasp the significance of the campaign and were reluctant to cooperate.

I didn't have any money. I managed to pay my travel expenses by selling off some personal belongings. Still, I was utterly resolved that we would be victorious. "I am the direct disciple of Josei Toda, a great mentor spearheading the development of our movement for kosen-rufu. There is absolutely no reason that I should not win!" With this thought, I would encourage myself to continue onward. I would not accept defeat! I would triumph! Such was my burning spirit as Mr. Toda's disciple.

The Record of the Orally Transmitted Teachings says: "If in a single moment of life we exhaust the pains and trials of millions of kalpas, then instant after instant there will arise in us the three Buddha bodies with which we are eternally endowed. [Chanting] Nam-myoho-renge-kyo is just such a 'diligent' practice" (OTT, 214). In accord with these words of Nichiren Daishonin, as long as we chant to win based on a spirit of unity with our mentor, boundless wisdom will well up from within and we will be able to bring forth the power of the Buddha. When we then confidently engage others in dialogue, we will be able to genuinely touch their lives and call forth their Buddha nature.

The second point I focused on was to chant united in prayer with my fellow members.

Most of those striving alongside me in Yamaguchi were new to the practice of Nichiren Buddhism. Members also came from all over Japan to support us. Many were struggling with serious personal problems, such as illness or financial difficulties. I chanted intensely that every one of them, without exception, would achieve a great and expansive state of life brimming with happiness and help others do the same. At every available opportunity, I did gongyo and recited the sutra and chanted Nam-myoho-renge-kyo together with the members striving in Yamaguchi.

How do you unite a diverse group of members? The key, the Daishonin says, is to chant daimoku together so that everyone can unite in the spirit of "many in body but one in mind, transcending all differences among themselves to become as inseparable as fish and the water in which they swim" (WND-1, 217). The "mind" in "many in body but one in mind" refers to faith. We need to unite in the great vow to realize kosen-rufu. People's wish to change their karma is also encompassed in that endeavor.

It is important that we support and encourage our fellow members, to share their joys and sufferings, and to chant together with them in a spirit of caring and empathy. When we join our prayers in this way, based on the clear and great goal of kosen-rufu, the strength of our unity multiplies exponentially.

The third point was to respond with lightning speed.

After Mr. Toda assigned me the responsibility of leading propagation efforts in Yamaguchi, I immediately began to gather information on the area and plan my schedule. I researched Yamaguchi's history, geography, and the character of the residents. I did this on my own, looking for a way to set our campaign in motion. I also set concrete goals for each visit there and strove with all my might to achieve them.

The goal for my first visit was to unite with the members in Yamaguchi and kick off our campaign. On the second visit, I aimed to make a breakthrough in our propagation efforts and invigorate the local organization. On the third visit, I sought to solidify our growth. In that way, I took steady, precise steps toward victory.

Acting with speed is proof that leaders are taking the initiative. When leaders are firmly resolved to allow no negative influences to affect them, they can take speedy and appropriate action.

Even when I wasn't physically in Yamaguchi, I was constantly thinking about the Yamaguchi members and their problems, and I encouraged them regularly with telephone calls and letters.

As leaders, it is crucial that we act swiftly and promptly, doing everything possible to encourage and inspire our fellow members.

In a letter to his youthful disciple Nanjo Tokimitsu, the Daishonin assures him that Shakyamuni, Many Treasures Buddha, the innumerable Buddhas and bodhisattvas, and the protective forces of the universe will "as a shadow follows a form, guard anyone who has firm faith in this Lotus Sutra [Nam-myoho-renge-kyo] and who remains at all times stalwart and unwavering in that faith" (WND-2, 638).

No one is stronger or more invincible than a youth who single-mindedly follows the path of mentor and disciple toward the achievement of kosen-rufu.

Determination, prayer, and action—this formula for victory has been inherited by our youth in Yamaguchi Prefecture and the rest of the Chugoku region, whose local Gakkai organization I personally devoted myself to building, as well as by youth throughout Japan and around the world.

—"Building a Network of Justice and Peace,"
in *World Tribune*, January 20, 2012, 5.

ARAKAWA CAMPAIGN

◆ ◆ ◆ ◆ ◆

August 1957

Introduction

◆ ◆ ◆ ◆ ◆

ARAKAWA WAS . . . a place of unforgettable memories for Shin'ichi. In 1957, just prior to becoming the Katsushika Ward greater block leader, he had spent seven days there from August 8 through 14 conducting a summer guidance session. Wherever he went during that time, whether on train platforms or on the neighborhood streets, he had engaged members in earnest dialogue, regarding each encounter as a once-in-a-lifetime opportunity.

His spirited cry "Let's work together to open a new age for Arakawa!" had inspired them all, and in one week, more than two hundred households had taken faith there, a more than 10 percent increase in membership for the ward at that time.

—"Heart and Soul" chapter, NHR-16, 83–84.

The Campaign

◆ ◆ ◆ ◆ ◆

STIRRING A GROUNDSWELL FOR PEOPLE'S VICTORY

Arakawa Ward was a down-to-earth neighborhood. The small homes crowded up against one another, and in the evening the air was filled with homey scents and sounds—the aroma and smoke of fish being grilled, the sounds of fans flapping in order to keep charcoal fires going, the rhythmic chopping of vegetables on cutting boards, the cries of infants, and the voices of mothers scolding their children.

Among the ward's residents, there were many who hailed from the Japanese countryside, including numerous young people who had come to the metropolis for work. They were honest, straightforward, and warmhearted—not the kind of people to put on airs or behave in an affected manner. Shin'ichi had a great fondness for Arakawa Ward.

As he made his way there for the summer block guidance tour, he resolved to himself that he would stir a groundswell for the people's victory from Arakawa, a place that epitomized the lives of ordinary people. He would build a bastion of truth and justice that no authority or power elite could destroy.

When he arrived at Chiyoko Tsuchida's house for the meeting, she was standing outside waiting for him. They went inside together, where about ten other members were already seated. Shin'ichi said, "Let's all chant for the great victory of Arakawa."

Their struggle began with prayer. Shin'ichi's clear voice resonated through the house. They solemnly recited the sutra, brimming with the sincere wish for victory. When it was over, Shin'ichi asked, "Where is Mr. Tsuchida?"

"Here I am," a man of about fifty sitting at the back of the room replied gruffly. It was Tamio Tsuchida.

Shin'ichi bowed deeply. "Pleased to meet you. My name is Shin'ichi Yamamoto. Thank you for your hospitality and for allowing us to use your home for our meeting today."

"It's nothing," said Tsuchida abashedly.

Under the line organization, Tsuchida was a vice district leader. His wife Chiyoko, however, was a chapter leader and was frequently away from home, which meant he looked after the house. Tamio often used to say that his wife was the center of their family and that his role was merely to support her. He was also rather passive when it came to Soka Gakkai activities.

Shin'ichi said to Tamio: "Why are you sitting all the way back there? Please come to the front of the room. If you're in the front here where everyone can see you, your guests will be more at ease. Please, come on up here." At Shin'ichi's encouragement, Tamio moved to the front of the room. "Here, sit next to me," Shin'ichi said.

Tamio reluctantly complied. At the same time, however, he appeared somewhat delighted.

"I'd like to ask that you make it a point of sitting in the front when you have a meeting in your house," Shin'ichi continued. "And at the next discussion meeting here, please make some opening remarks and welcome everyone to your home. Doing so will put those members visiting for the first time, as well as invited guests, at ease. Will you do that for me?"

"Yes." And at that moment, the feeling of being a mere bystander evaporated from his heart.

The success of any activity starts with each member becoming a protagonist. It is not that certain people have special abilities; by making an earnest effort, everyone can be a great leader. That is why it is so important to wholeheartedly encourage each person we meet. . . .

"Let's engage in a great effort to introduce as many people as possible to Nichiren Buddhism here in Arakawa Ward, a microcosm of the people and the Soka Gakkai, and build a golden citadel of the kosen-rufu movement in eastern Japan. Join me in creating a wonderful and everlasting history of the people's victory!"

"We will!" everyone replied, their eyes shining with determination.

"All right. It's decided. Arakawa will be victorious. If we're in earnest, we can overcome any obstacle." . . .

The conversation then moved on to considering the detailed plans for Shin'ichi's guidance tour. Eventually, they decided that the ward would be divided into five areas with one person responsible for each. They also resolved whose home would serve as the base for their activities, as well as the discussion meeting schedule.

When all the planning was completed, Shin'ichi said: "In order to achieve unprecedented expansion in this short one-week period, we'll need to muster great wisdom. I'm sure you're all thinking about how many people you introduced to Buddhism last month and the month before, and you may even feel that you've reached the limit and that there are no more people to share Nichiren Buddhism with. Such thinking, however, is actually an obstacle.

"But where does that obstacle exist? It exists in our own mind. We create it ourselves. The fact is that there are many people around us we could talk to about Buddhism—we just haven't made an opportunity to speak with them or we haven't engaged them in deep dialogue.

"That's where wisdom comes in—the wisdom to figure out how we can start the dialogue, how we can strike a chord in the other person's heart. We need to muster all our wisdom to find answers to these questions."

The members listened intently as Shin'ichi spoke, nodding in understanding.

Gazing at the face of each person in the room, [he] continued: "After talking to a person just once, you may find yourself jumping to the conclusion that he or she isn't receptive and that you'll never get anywhere with the person. But people's minds are always changing, minute by minute, and you can definitely change them through your persevering efforts at dialogue.

"Sometimes, we need to consider whether our manner of speaking might be at fault. For example, if we tell a person with family problems that they can overcome illness through Buddhism, we're not going to pique their interest. Likewise, it doesn't do much good to tell a person struggling with illness that faith will help them succeed in business. Employing wisdom also means determining how to gain the other person's understanding.

"Some members may have many friends but, lacking conviction, are unable to talk about faith persuasively. In such cases, it's a good idea to have a senior in faith support that person in talking to their friends about Buddhism.

"Our wisdom is essentially unlimited. It can make the impossible possible. And it arises from the firm resolve to achieve something. Earnest prayer is the mother of wisdom."

Shin'ichi went on to say that wisdom needed to be accompanied by the courage to put it into action: "As Nichiren Daishonin writes, 'A sword is useless in the hands of a coward' (WND-1, 412). The sword of the Lotus Sutra, which is the source of limitless wisdom, has no power if we are cowardly.

"I hope you will have the courage to challenge and overcome your personal weaknesses, such as the tendency to avoid the things you don't like and to make excuses to justify your cowardice and negativity. Doing so is the key to your human revolution and to victory in all your endeavors." . . .

Shin'ichi's activities in Arakawa began. Only a week in length, the summer block guidance tour was a struggle against time. Spending each moment valuably was therefore crucial in determining victory, while a moment's carelessness could be the cause for irreparable defeat.

Shin'ichi Yamamoto exerted himself wholeheartedly in visiting the neighborhoods of Arakawa Ward, including Nippori, Ogu, Machiya, and Minami-Senju. He approached each discussion meeting he attended as if it were an all-out struggle. Every meeting place was packed to overflowing and the members were brimming with enthusiasm. . . .

Shin'ichi addressed the members' questions at all the discussion meetings he attended. He knew that the members would gain the momentum to advance if he answered their questions clearly and gave them courage and hope. On one occasion, a men's division member said: "I'm a unit leader, but when I hold unit meetings, very few people come and the gatherings are hardly inspiring. What should I do?"

"May I ask if you are married?"

"Yes, I am," replied the man. "My wife is also a member."

"I see," Shin'ichi said. "Well, you can have a discussion meeting with just you and your wife. First, try to have the very best discussion meeting possible by yourselves. Then, with shared determination, go out to visit the members in your unit and invite them to attend the next meeting. If you are inclined to depend on others, you'll be defeated. Not taking the initiative is a cause for failure."

The man's expression showed that Shin'ichi's words had struck home.

Shin'ichi continued: "Nichiren Daishonin says, 'If a commanding general is fainthearted, his soldiers will become cowards' (WND-1, 464). The point is to stand up and take the lead, to be resolved that you will win even if you have to do it on your own. That determination, that spirit, will definitely inspire others.

"During this current campaign, try putting this spirit into practice. If you are able to break through your own limitations, your unit discussion meetings will be a success and you will exhibit tremendous strength in your other Buddhist activities as well as in your work. Faith is manifested in daily life. If your basic attitude in faith changes, your work situation and life will too."

Shin'ichi did his utmost to respond to each member's question, no matter what it was. He regarded the exchanges as opportunities to awaken fresh resolve in people and enable them to transform their life. This was his spirit, whether the person was an adult or a child.

On one occasion, Shin'ichi was a little late arriving for a discussion meeting in Minami-Senju, having spent more time than he anticipated talking to someone about practicing Buddhism. As he

approached the meeting place, he saw a group of young people standing in the street waiting for him. The daughter of the family at whose home the meeting was being held was with them. Her name was Ikuko Tabata, and she was in the fifth grade of elementary school.

When Ikuko saw Shin'ichi, she said, "Sensei, you're late!"

"I'm very sorry," Shin'ichi replied. "I was busy talking to someone about Nichiren Buddhism and was slightly delayed."

Shin'ichi walked the rest of the way to the house with Ikuko.

During the meeting, he fielded questions, saying: "If you have anything you'd like to ask, please go ahead. It doesn't have to be about faith. It can be about history or literature, too, for example."

After several members had asked questions about their personal struggles, Ikuko raised her hand. "Sensei!" she called out. "Was Joan of Arc a real person?"

It was a question out of the blue, and some of the members gave the girl a strange look. Shin'ichi, however, smiled and nodded. With a heartfelt wish for Ikuko's growth, he earnestly proceeded to answer her question. He said: "Yes, she was. She was a girl who lived in France in the fifteenth century. She led an army to protect her country, drove out the English forces and liberated Orléans, which had been surrounded by the invaders. But her end was tragic, and she was burned at the stake while still a teenager. So you are far more fortunate than her. Nevertheless, her spirit to give her life for the sake of others and for the people's happiness was truly great. I hope that you will have the same spirit throughout your life and strive tirelessly for the people's welfare and for peace, finding your own happiness at the same time. Please promise me you'll become a Joan of Arc of the Mystic Law."

"I promise!" Ikuko said resolutely, her eyes shining with determination.

When the discussion meeting was over, Shin'ichi looked at Ikuko and said, "Goodbye, Joan of Arc!" Ikuko cherished Shin'ichi's guidance throughout her life. She firmly vowed to become a Joan of Arc of the Mystic Law, working for the happiness of all people. In later years, she became a nationwide young women's division leader and then a women's division leader. She intrepidly led the

way on the front lines of the kosen-rufu movement, holding aloft the banner of the people's victory. . . .

Shin'ichi's summer guidance tour in Arakawa was only a week long, but he approached every moment with great passion and enthusiasm. His dedicated actions inspired members anew in their endeavors for kosen-rufu. . . .

Each evening, members came to the Tsuchida family home, the base of activities in Arakawa, to report on the results of their propagation efforts. In the end, the members were successful in introducing Nichiren Buddhism to more than two hundred new households in Arakawa Ward.

—"Citadel of the People" chapter, NHR-17, 207–18.

Lessons
Inspired by the Mentor

◆ ◆ ◆ ◆ ◆ ◆

WHAT WAS THE DRIVING FORCE FOR THE ARAKAWA CAMPAIGN?

Shin'ichi had fond memories of Arakawa Ward, having led a summer block guidance tour there in August 1957.

The area had changed considerably. Some tall buildings now stood along the main avenue, but there were still enough of the older buildings to bring back old memories as he looked out of the car window.

The white building of the Arakawa Culture Center was already taking on an impressive form. As it came into view, Shin'ichi said, gazing out of the window: "What a wonderful culture center! It's truly a citadel of the people in a town of the people." . . .

One of the leaders accompanying Shin'ichi asked: "During the

Arakawa summer block guidance tour that you led in August 1957, you achieved a 10 percent increase in membership—more than two hundred new households—in just a single week. I was wondering, what was the driving force for that campaign?"

Shin'ichi replied without hesitation: "It was the single-minded wish for each person to become happy. At that time, everyone was overwhelmed by their own karma—struggling with problems such as poverty, unemployment, sickness, and family discord.

"I met members and continually tried to impress upon them that the only way for them to break through and transform their karma was to awaken to their mission as Bodhisattvas of the Earth and make great efforts for kosen-rufu.

"Though the period of the campaign was brief, the members chanted intensely with the determination that they would use the campaign to share Nichiren Buddhism with many others and to overcome their problems. They challenged their problems courageously and strove all out. They made efforts not because they had been told to but because they were driven by a fighting spirit that welled up from the depths of their lives.

"The purpose of our faith and Soka Gakkai activities is to become happy. They're all for our own benefit, which in turn leads to prosperity in society.

"Throughout the campaign and afterward as well, I received reports from many members about the benefit they experienced in having surmounted their hardships.

"Leaders must never forget that the Soka Gakkai's triumphant history is nothing other than our members' victory of having deepened their conviction in Buddhism and developed a sense of real joy and happiness."

The leaders accompanying Shin'ichi felt as if they had been reminded of an extremely important point that had been forgotten.

"Moreover, the main reason that I was able to fully exert myself in Arakawa Ward," Shin'ichi continued, "was my resolve to show proof of the Soka Gakkai's growth and development to reassure Mr. Toda about the future of kosen-rufu."

Shin'ichi remembered how he had felt at the time. Pursing his lips tightly, he looked into the distance. Then, as if he were choosing his words carefully, he began to speak slowly and with deep feeling: "The summer of that year, Mr. Toda fell ill, the strain of the Yubari Coal Miners Incident and the Osaka Incident taking a toll on his health. As the membership had reached 600,000 households at the end of June, the attainment of Mr. Toda's lifetime goal of 750,000 members was within sight.

"Achieving a membership of 750,000 households was the struggle of Mr. Toda's final years. I was determined for us to achieve it within 1957 so that his mind would be at ease.

"I resolved to become the driving force for its accomplishment.

And at the same time, I wanted to create an example of how kosen-rufu should be expanded on into the future.

"The final struggle of the mentor's life is to make sure that the disciples are achieving great victories. As disciples, therefore, it is important that we show actual proof so that we can proudly report to our mentor: 'I have triumphed!' This is the oneness of mentor and disciple.

"Because I had made up my mind in this way, I was able to tap my full strength; I was able to bring forth courage and wisdom.

"When we rise up as disciples with the eager determination to respond to our mentor in kosen-rufu, the same intrepid life state as our mentor will pulse in our own lives.

"This means, when we live with the awareness that mentor and disciple are one, we manifest the life state of the Bodhisattvas of the Earth, who vowed in the distant past to take on the great mission of kosen-rufu together with their teacher. We will be filled with incomparable strength."

—"Bold Advance" chapter, NHR-26, 314–18.

Youth, Open a New Age of Kosen-rufu in Your Communities

In both my summer block guidance campaign in Arakawa, and my subsequent efforts as Katsushika greater block leader, I emphasized home visits and personal guidance to establish strong ties with individual members.

Before and after meetings, wanting to make the most of every moment, I went to visit one member after another at their homes. When I only had time for a short chat at the door, I always promised to stop by again. Making a note of everyone's name and address, I often sent them postcards later with an encouraging message.

I also held informal meetings and question-and-answer sessions, so that members could get to know me and one another. I listened to young men's division members having trouble at work and men's division members with family problems. I chanted with them and encouraged them with all my heart.

I was in earnest. I tried my hardest. I wanted everyone to fully savor the joy of practicing Nichiren Daishonin's teachings.

All people have a mission that is theirs and theirs alone. All are capable individuals; all are comrades who share profound karmic connections.

The way to foster people is to meet people. It is important to actively reach out to and engage with others. Steady, ongoing, grassroots activities—discussion meetings, home visits, personal guidance, question-and-answer sessions, informal meetings—are the key to victory. The SGI has been successful in its endeavors because of this solid track record of steady, consistent efforts, like flowing water. This formula will never change—and, I would like to say, we must never allow it to change.

Kosen-rufu in our local areas is a movement to spread joy and hope toward life throughout our communities. We who uphold the Mystic Law are responsible for the happiness of our communities; we are the pioneers.

Through Nichiren Daishonin's sincere encouragement, Nanjo Tokimitsu grew into a leader of kosen-rufu in Suruga Province. In the same way, let us open a new age of kosen-rufu in our communities with youth in the lead. . . .

May our youth . . . stand up to play a leading role for the happiness and welfare of their communities!

—*The Teachings for Victory*, vol. 4 (Santa Monica, CA:
World Tribune Press, 2017), 111–12.

CREATING A TRADITION OF
UNDEFEATED VICTORY

After arriving at the Arakawa Culture Center, Shin'ichi . . . talked
with the Arakawa members and listened intently as they told him
about their activities. When the subject turned to his leadership
in the Arakawa campaign in August 1957, Shin'ichi said, "During
that campaign, I set out with fellow pioneer members to accomplish a deliberately challenging goal, and together we created a
record that established Arakawa as a champion. Through that
struggle, everyone deeply engraved in their lives the powerful
conviction that when we take on and overcome difficult challenges for kosen-rufu, we will savor the joy and exhilaration of
winning and forge a state of indestructible happiness.

"More than two decades have gone by since then. I'd now like
each of you to create a new record of victory based on that tradition and pass that legacy on to the next generation.

"But we can't create or maintain a tradition of victory in our movement for kosen-rufu just by doing the same old thing. Both the times and society change. It's by staying creative and innovative, continually taking on fresh challenges and succeeding in every endeavor that a lasting tradition of victory is formed. What we need to convey to the next generation is that fighting spirit."

The spirit to fight for kosen-rufu is a legacy that cannot be transmitted through words alone. It is passed along from senior to junior, from one person to another, through shared experience and a process of inspiration while striving together in Soka Gakkai activities.

With high hopes, Shin'ichi said, "Now is the time for each of you here in Arakawa to fight valiantly in the same spirit as me. If a tradition of undefeated victory is established in a single area, the Soka Gakkai will flourish forever, because everyone will learn from that example. I hope you'll always remember that this is the great mission of Arakawa." . . .

The members' eyes sparkled with determination.

—"Awaiting the Time" chapter, NHR-30, 170–72.
World Tribune, March 1, 2019, 7–8.